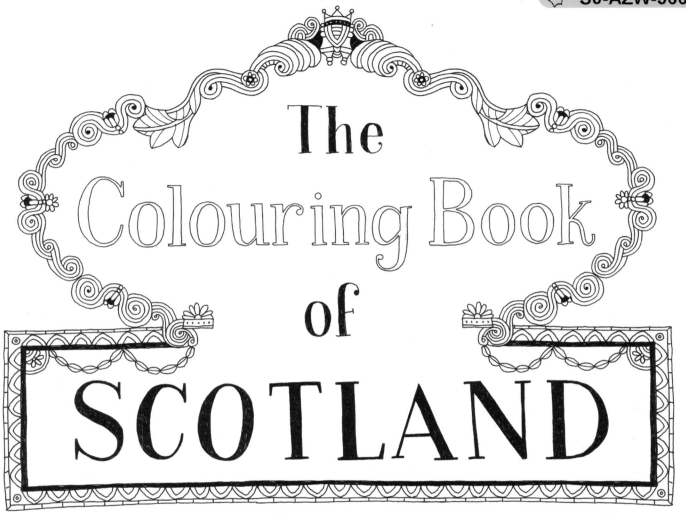

The Colouring Book of SCOTLAND

by
Eilidh Muldoon

BIRLINN

Edinburgh Castle

The Forth Bridge

St Andrews

Balmoral Castle

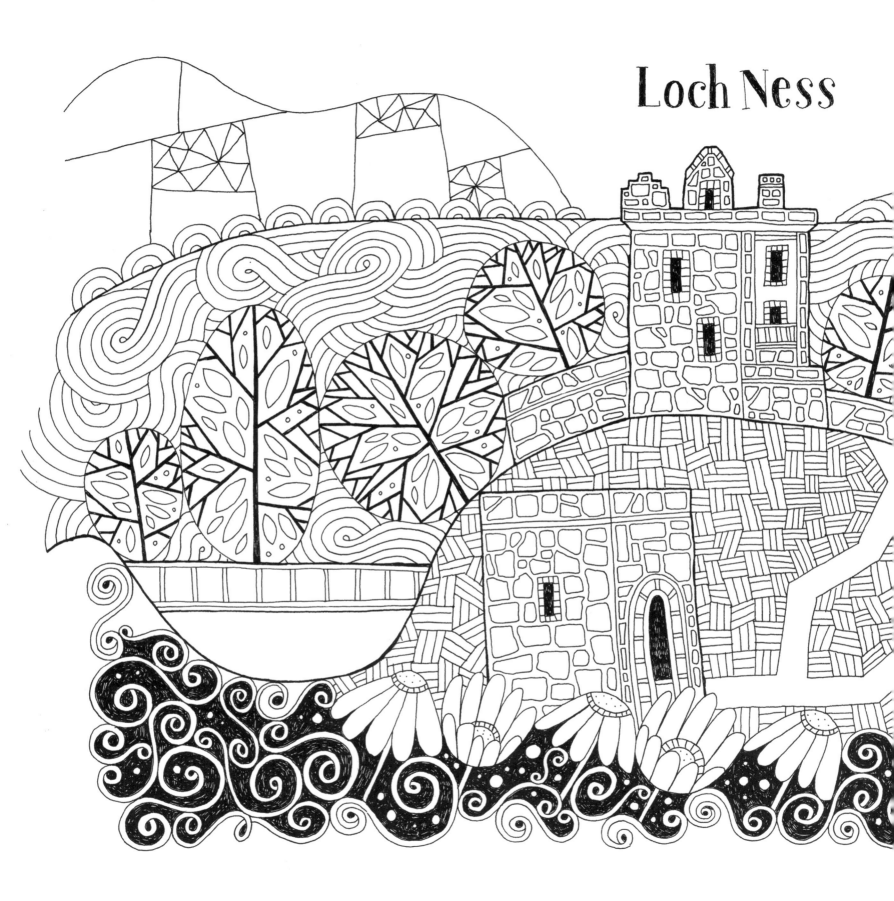

Loch Ness

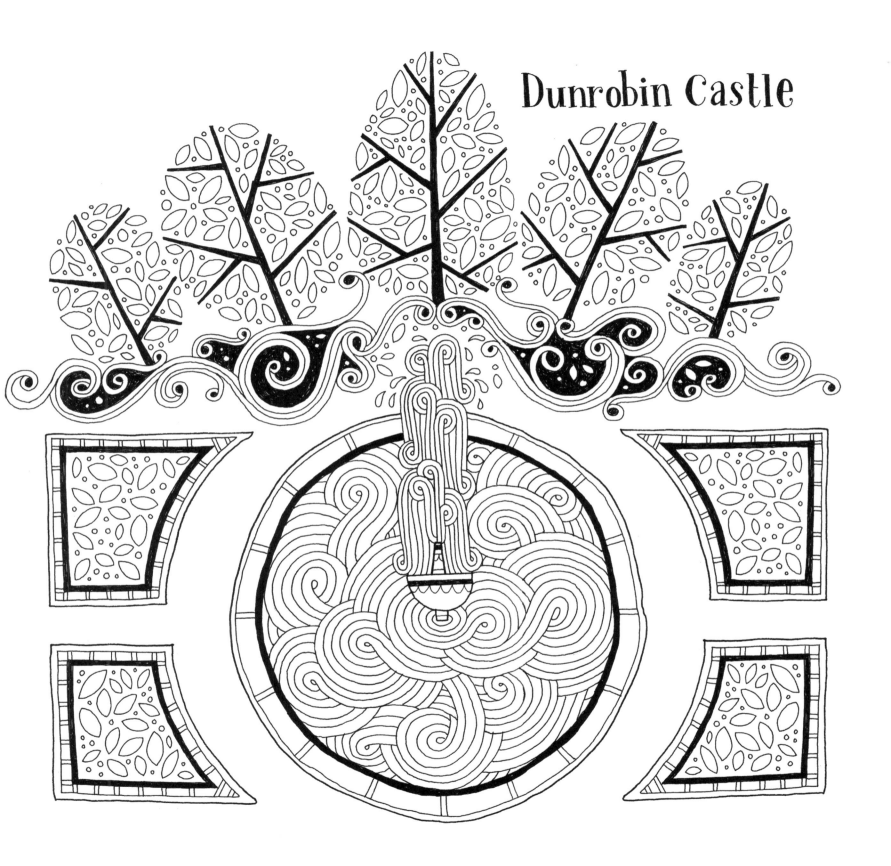

Dunrobin Castle

Stromness

Skara Brae

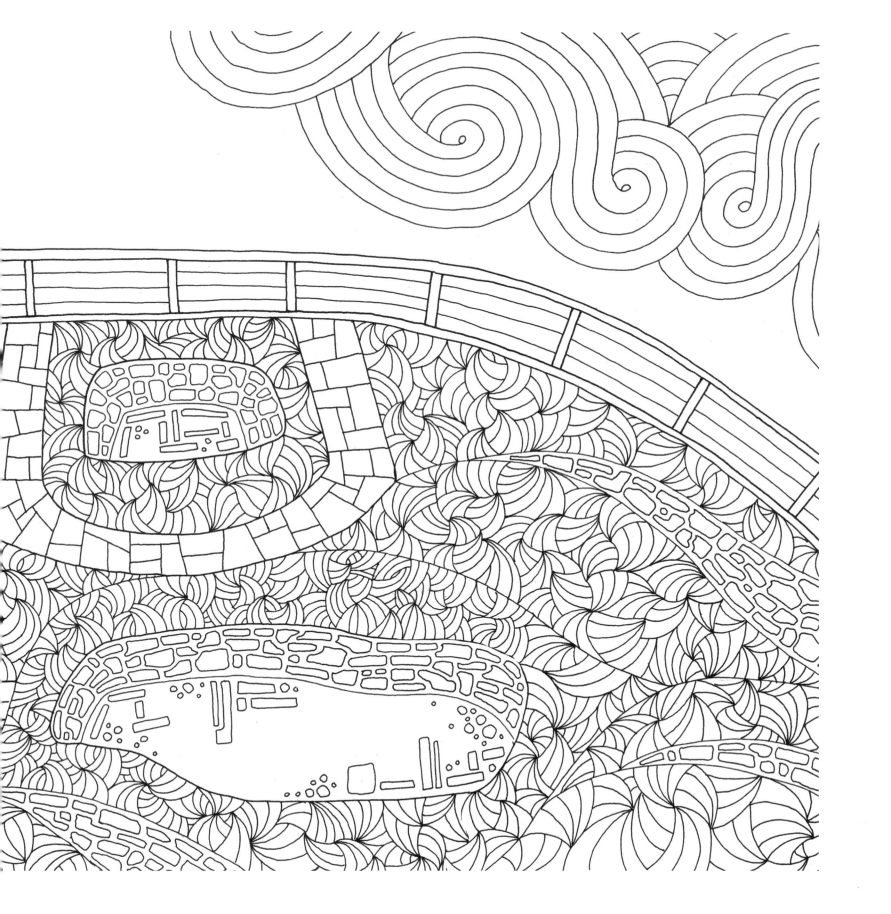

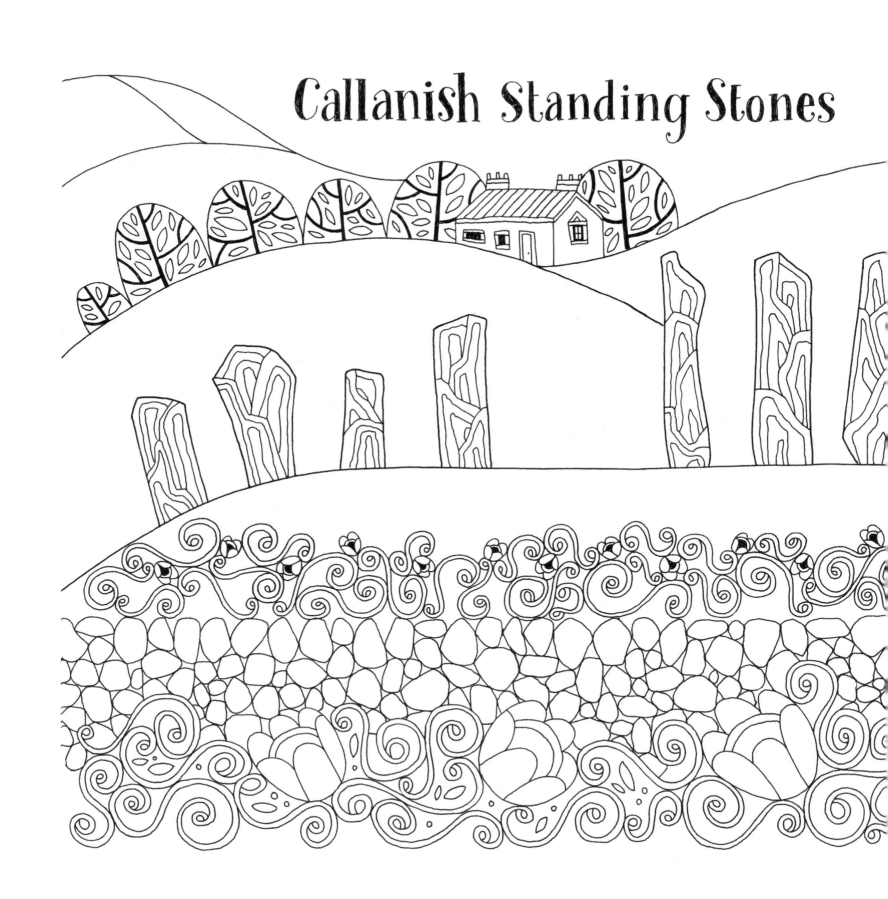

Callanish Standing Stones

Stornoway

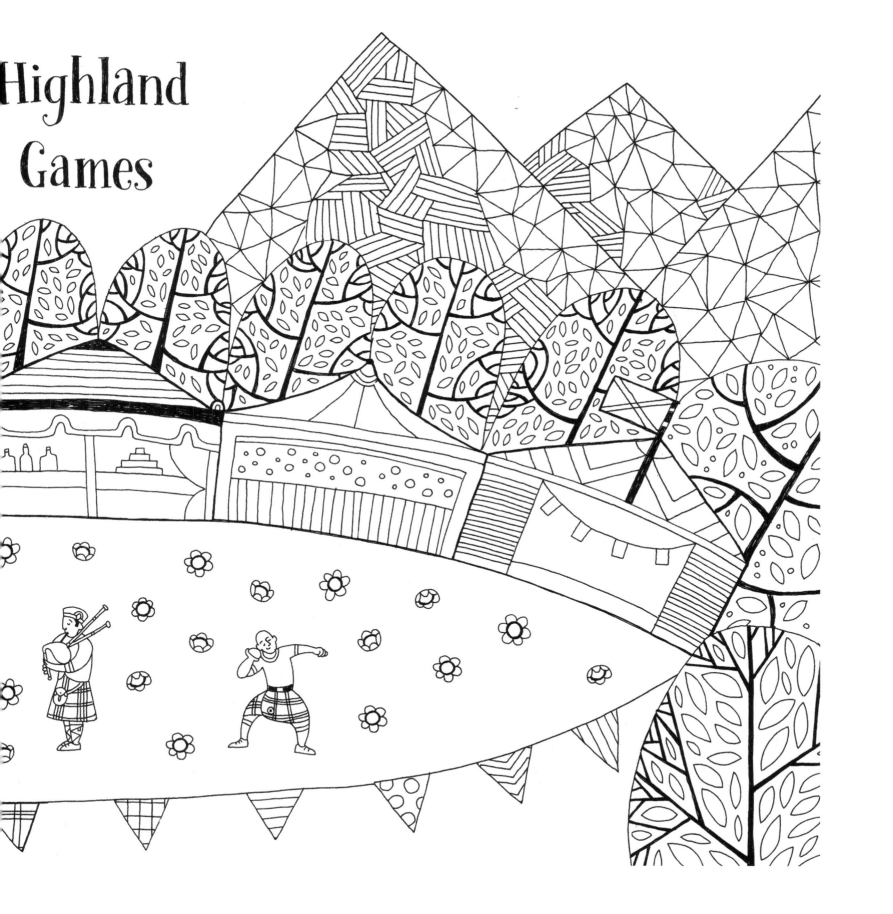

Highland Games

Eilean Donan

Duart Castle

KELVINGROVE A

Kelvingrove

RY AND MUSEUM

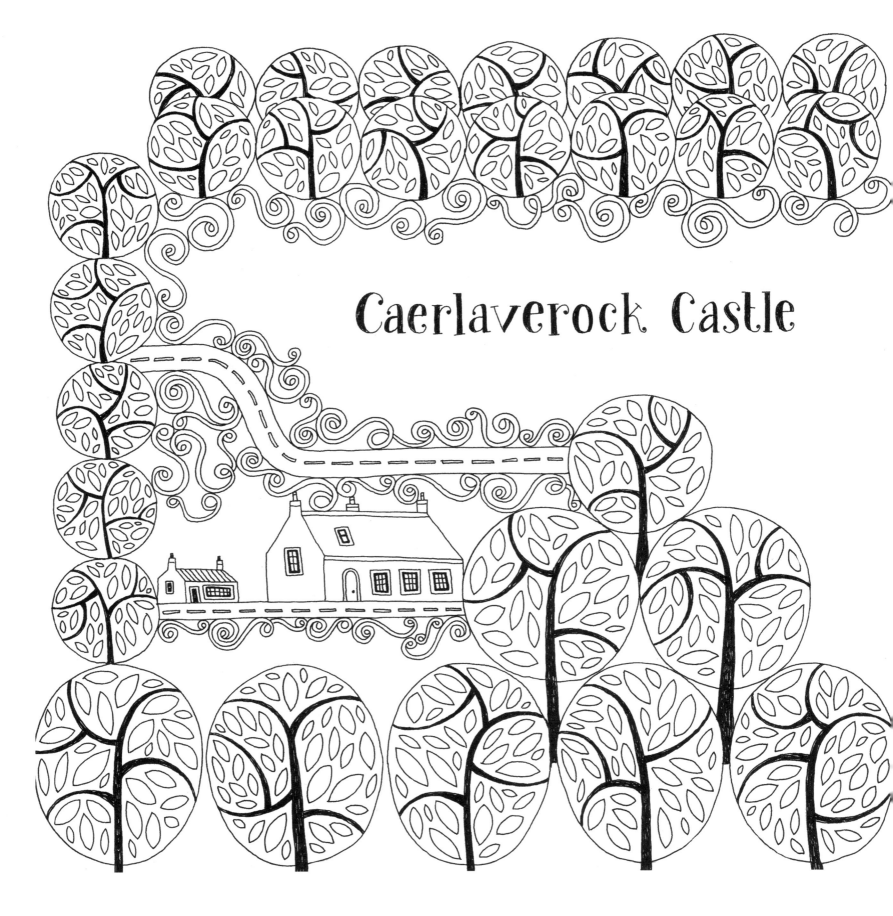

Caerlaverock Castle

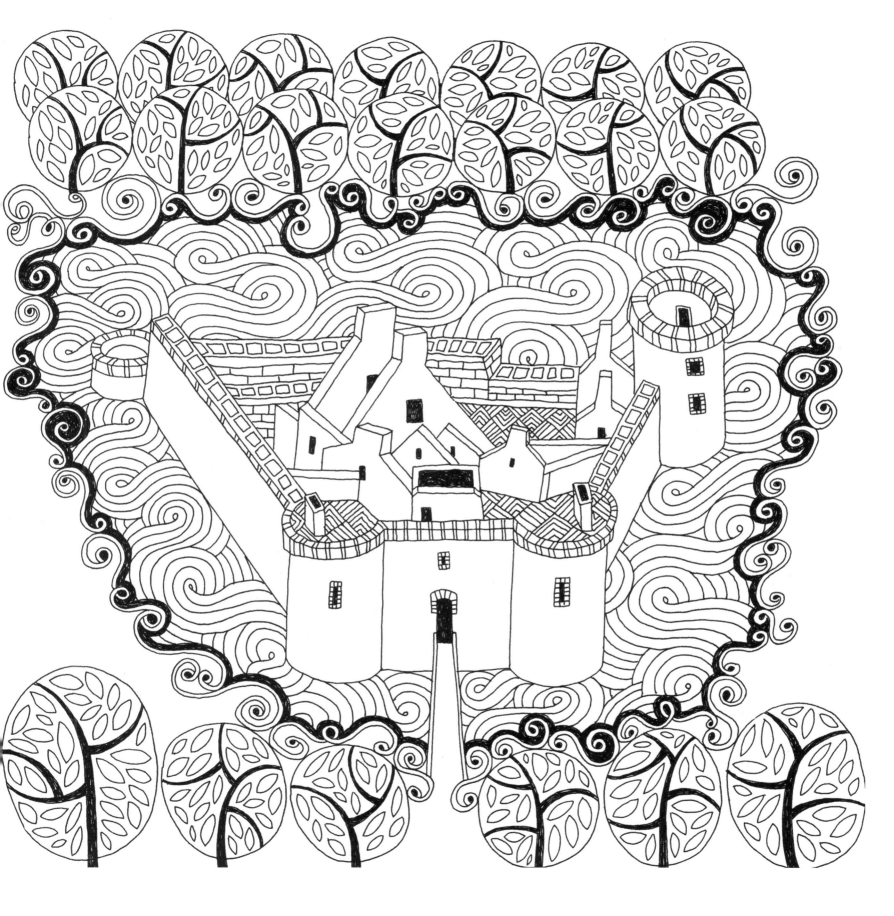

Abbotsford

Melrose Abbey

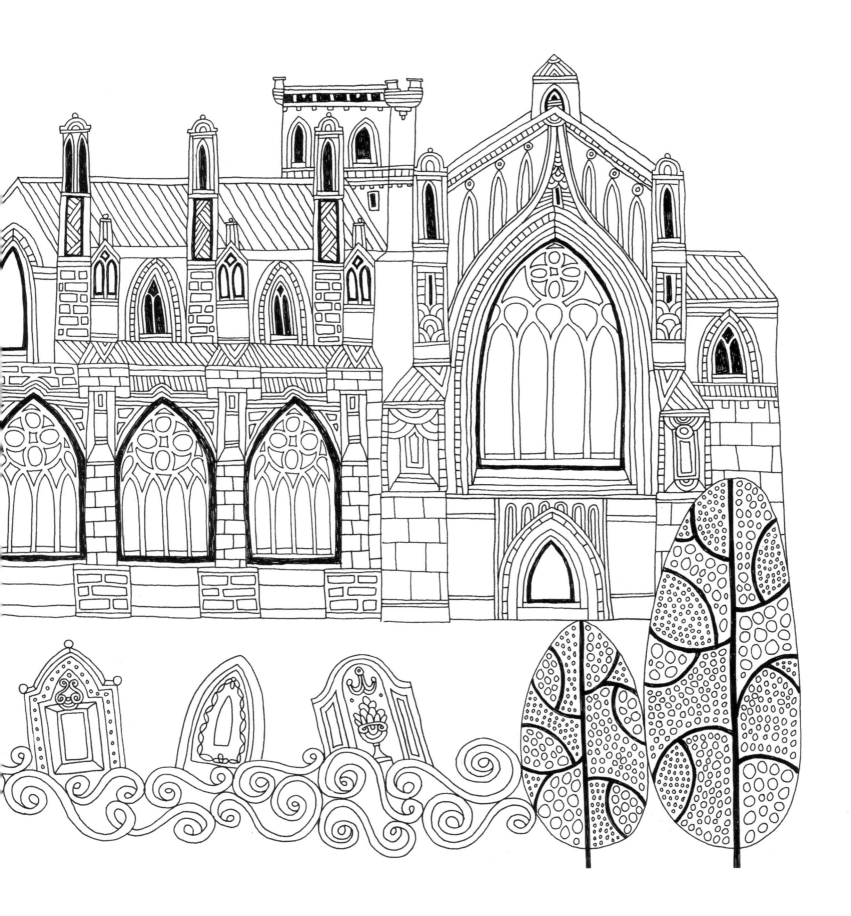

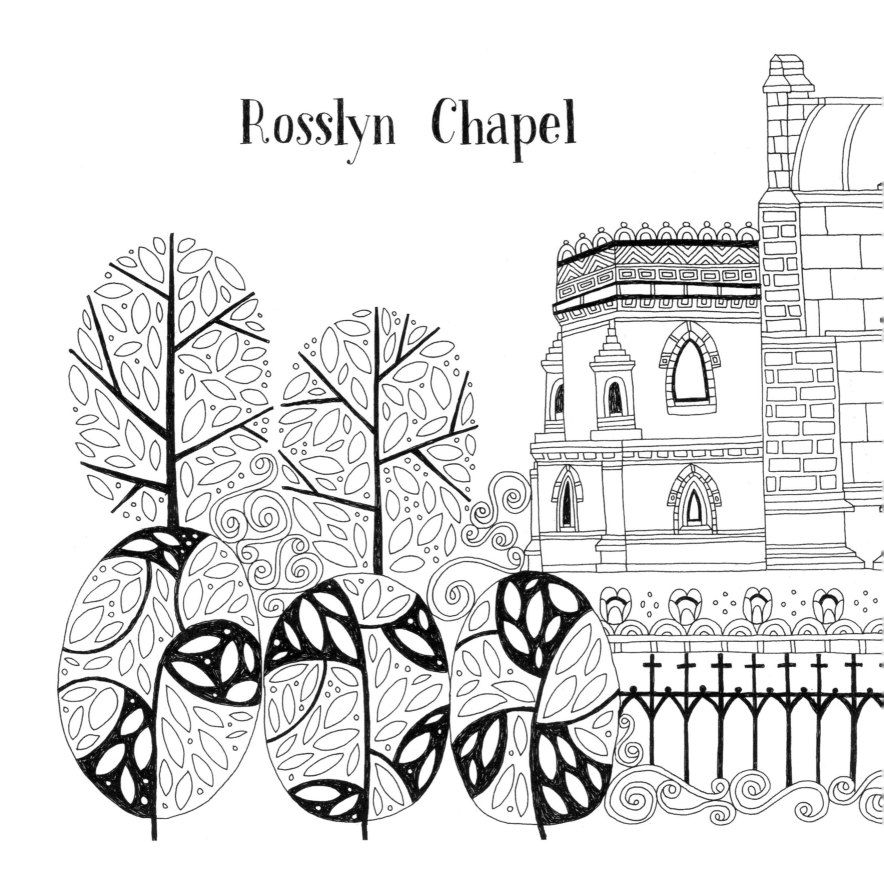

Rosslyn Chapel

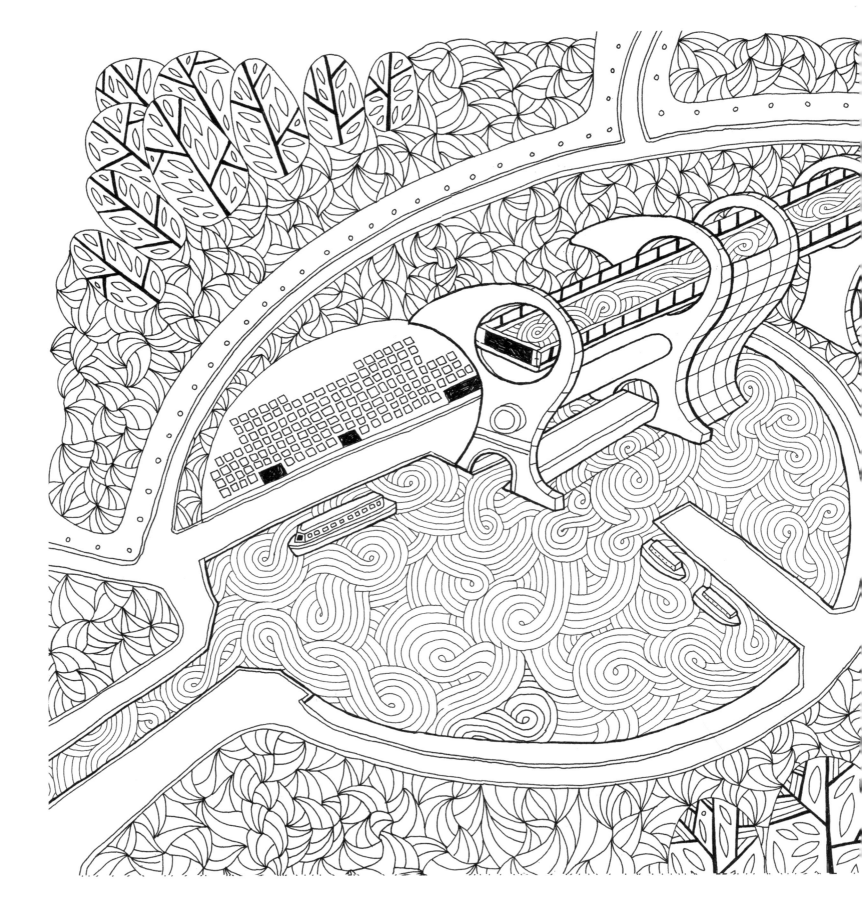

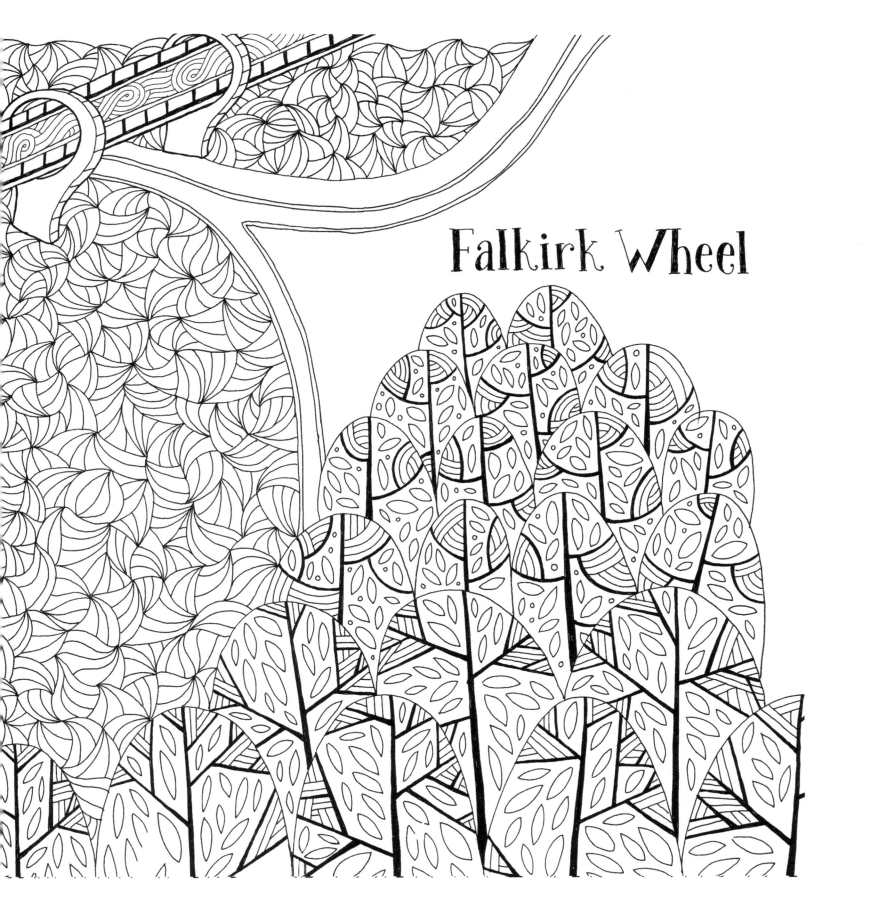

Falkirk Wheel

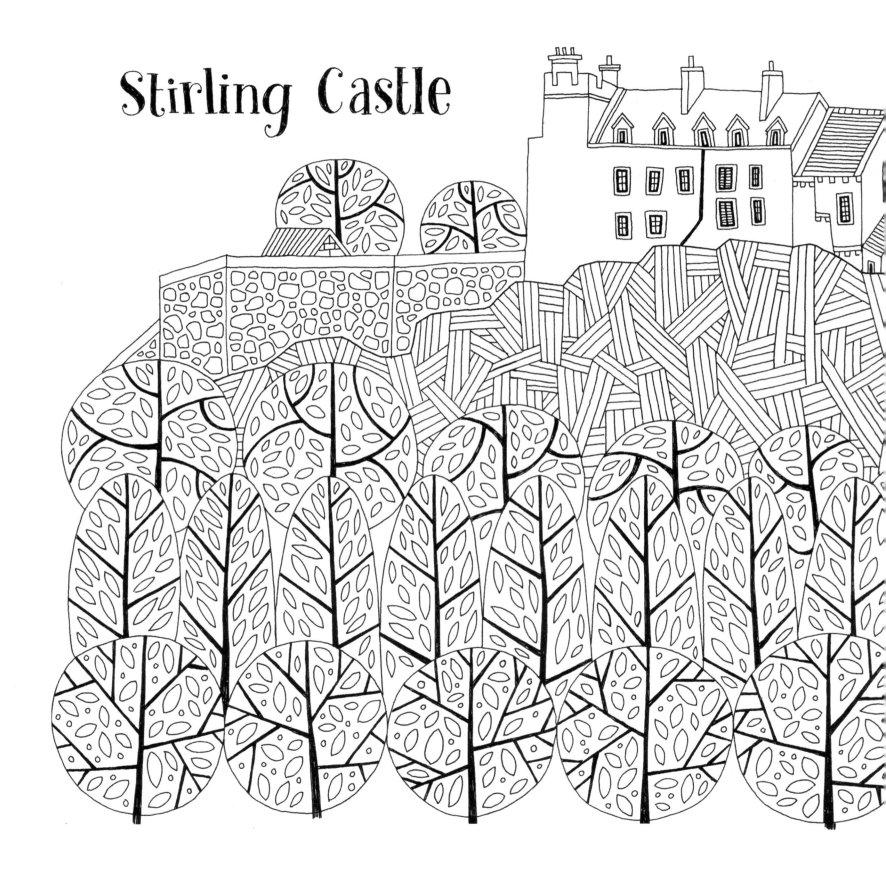

Stirling Castle

The Colouring Book of SCOTLAND
Journey

One: Edinburgh Castle
Two: The Forth Bridge
Three: St Andrews, Fife
Four: RRS Discovery, Dundee
Five: Balmoral, Royal Deeside
Six: Loch Ness
Seven: Dunrobin Castle, Golspie
Eight: Stromness, Orkney
Nine: Skara Brae, Orkney
Ten: Callanish Stones, Isle of Lewis
Eleven: Stornoway, Isle of Lewis
Twelve: Highland Games
Thirteen: Eilean Donan, Kyle of Lochalsh
Fourteen: Duart Castle, Isle of Mull
Fifteen: Tobermory, Isle of Mull
Sixteen: Kelvingrove Gallery, Glasgow
Seventeen: Caerlaverock Castle, Dumfries
Eighteen: Abbotsford, Melrose
Nineteen: Melrose Abbey, Melrose
Twenty: Rosslyn Chapel, Midlothian
Twenty-One: Falkirk Wheel
Twenty-Two: Stirling Castle
Twenty-Three: Edinburgh Christmas